Real Estate

Acknowledgements

I would like to thank my family for their love and support, especially my parents, who gave up so much for us to be in the United States. I am 'still humbled' by what my mom and dad had to do in order for us to have a better life here. I also wanted to thank my wife, kids, brother and sisters who supported me through good and rough times.

I also want to thank all of our team for sharing their insights and their willingness to collaborate with us to make every project a success. I do not believe in a one-man show and I would not have been here without the support of my team, family and friends. Thank you all for all you have done with me and for me.

Love,

Rock

Do not read this book unless you are ready to take action!

TABLE OF CONTENTS

Introduction

The economy in recent years has been so volatile that concerns about having an adequate retirement buffer have reached a pinnacle over the past decade. Social Security has lost its luster and does not look anywhere near being healthy enough to be able to provide for retirement in the future. These factors have been driving the rate of the ordinary person transforming into independent investors rapidly. The average person has started to take charge of their own financial futures. These new investors are looking for the magical swirling ship that will take them on a long and happy retirement cruise. The question remains however, "What type of investment will be able to sustain retirement or better still, yield the best returns in the long run?"

Some say its gold investment, some say it's the stock market and some even say oil and gas. The truth of the matter is however it is and has always been real estate. Take for example the stock market situation; the stock market is nothing more than a façade for gambling. It is a financial institution where nothing is concrete, solid or tangible. Governments have gone bankrupt due to the volatile nature of the stock market. People tend to speculate on stock prices just as a gambler would speculate what he dice will be rolling next on a roulette table. People have made fortunes from the stock market and this fact is undeniable, but more have lost everything they had due to it as well. The stock market is a coin flip, either you will make or you might end up losing all your savings.

Gold is another investment that people claim to be an asset sealing assurance. Is it really? In 1900 the amount of chickens you could buy with an ounce of gold is the same amount of chickens (maybe a few chickens more) you would be able to buy today. That is one hundred and thirteen years later. You get nothing more than you had. Investment is supposed to yield ''profitable returns" meaning if you invested in an ounce of gold a hundred years ago you should have at least double the returns such as two ounces of gold. To be blunt you get better returns from a banks fixed deposit investment. As for oil and gas, there will be no Oil and gas in the next hundred years!

When it comes to real estate however, it is a different ballgame altogether. If you invest in a single property, make some changes, add some color and paint, rest assured you will make a higher return in a very short time before the economy has a chance to cause any damage to the value of the home. Also if you intend to invest for the long run you may rent it out for a certain period of time (which is also revenue on investment) and if the economy does collapse, you could just wait it out and sell it when the economy recovers and still make a huge profit. The key reason behind this is real estate or properties do not declare themselves 'bankrupt' only people and companies. Worst case scenario, you can live in that property and save rent. Any which way you look at it, with real estate you win.

Notes:

_____

_____

_____

_____

_____

_____

6 C's

The six criterion of real estate that is a forte:

1. It allows you to earn dependable revenue through rentals

2. The value of real estate increases through appreciation ·

3. Objectively towards mortgage payoff (amortization)

4. Value adding via property improvement or modification

5. Instant profit through negotiation of reduction in purchase price

6. Government benefits through tax credits, tax deductions, rent vouchers, advantageous loans, etc.

Taking Notes in Summary of The 6 C's

- Rent & Revenue

_____

_____

- Appreciation & Profit

_____

_____

- Objective & Liability to Asset Conversion (Mortgage payoff)

- Value Adding & Increasing Profitability

- Negotiation & Instant profit

- Government Subsidies & Added Advantage

Real estate is also known as LADIES and LADIES stand for:

L = Leverage
A = Appreciation
D = Depreciation

I = Income
E = Equity
S = Security

From here we will seek to advance into what we may be able to safely deem as viable investments. We will wrestle with the question, "How can you evaluate an individual investment opportunity?" The answer to this question will then be forwarded to a comparison analysis that we will conduct on typical investment in small income properties versus investments in stocks and commodities. From the rationale we derive from this experiment you will be able to visualize on how real estate is a safer, more solid and secure as an investment compared to any other ventures. Experienced investors scrutinize any investment opportunities at its base. This base is basic survival 101.

Scribble Box

RELATIVE PRICE – YIELD – RISK

What is relative price?

_____

What is Yield?

_____

What is risk predominantly?

_____

Real estate investing involves the purchase, ownership, management, rental and sale of real estate for a return on investment (profit).

On another not the improvement of realty property is the part of the real estate investment strategy. In general it is considered a sub avenue in real estate investment that is referred to as real estate development. Real estate is an asset form with limited liquidity in relation to other primary investment. Real estate investment is also capital intensive albeit that capital may be harnessed via mortgage leverage and it is also highly cash flow dependent. If these factors are not well understood and managed by the investor, real estate becomes a risky investment. The primary cause of investment failure for real estate is that the investor goes into negative cash flow for a period of time that is not sustainable, often forcing them to resell the property at a loss or go into insolvency. A similar practice known as flipping is another reason for failure as the nature of the investment is often associated with short term profit with less effort.

The First Step – Identifying Real Estate

Identifying a real estate for the purpose of investment is a crucial if not vital step in the process of acquiring a property that is fit for investment purposes. However, this task requires due diligence and homework. For investors to purchase individual properties may be highly variable depending on knowledge of availability.

Information asymmetries are a commonplace in real estate markets to increase the understanding of the venture you are about to indulge in. Although this increases risk of being led in a different direction, with carefully calculated advancements it may be able to provide many opportunities for investors to obtain properties at bargain prices. Those who have been in the real estate industry for a period of time typically use a variety of techniques to determine the value of properties prior to purchase (Evaluation).

Step 2 Evaluations and Negotiation

Once an investment property has been located and preliminary investigation and verification of the condition and status of the property has been completed, the investor will have to negotiate a sale price and sale terms with the seller, then execute a contract for sale. Most investors employ real estate agents and real estate legal experts to assist with the acquisition process due to the complexities of the process that is involved. During the acquisition of a property, an investor will typically make a formal offer to buy including payment of "earnest money" to the seller at the start of negotiation to reserve the investor's rights to complete the transaction if price and terms can be satisfactorily negotiated. This earnest money may or may not be refundable, and is considered to be a signal of the seriousness of the investor's intent to purchase. The terms of the offer will also usually include a number of clauses which allow the investor time to complete due diligence, inspect the property and obtain financing among other requirements prior to final purchase. Within the contingency period, the investor usually withholds the right to rescind the offer with no penalty and obtain a refund of earnest money deposits. Once contingencies have expired, rescinding the offer will usually require forfeiture of the earnest money deposits and may involve other penalties as well.

Notes:

_____

_____

_____

Frequently Asked Questions (FAQs)

Question:
What does hassle free investing mean?

Answer:
We provide you with deeply discounted properties (60% - 70% of the market value with all repairs completed) that provide you with a monthly check from the rental income.

Each property will be fully repaired.
We will locate a tenant buyer to occupy the property. We will manage the tenant and the property. The tenant-owner has been informed that all minor repairs (up to $300) have to be handled by him/her (the major repairs have already been handled by us). We will help the tenant buyer to improve their credit so we can cash in the equity as soon as we can.

Question:

What is the potential gain?

Answer:

Using our model, you can double the income from your original investment from the rental income in 2 years (even assuming 3 months of vacancy) and you can double your original investment when we sell the property.

Note: Due to regulatory issues, all income claims are representative and cannot be guaranteed.

Scribble Box

Question:
The real estate market and stock market seem very unsteady right now. Why shouldn't I wait?

Answer:
Historically, more money is made in down markets because of the great bargains available. Billionaire J. Paul Getty once said: "I buy when there's blood on the street." Warren Buffett, the world's richest man, is also on a shopping spree right now as well. He also said, "Be greedy when others are fearful and be fearful when others are greedy". When the market is appreciating, the prices are so over inflated it's almost impossible to get a good return (this is the reason why so many folks have lost money in real estate – they bought at the peak of the market). The key to wealth building is being a contrarian's investor.

_____

_____

Question:
If the deals are so great, why aren't you keeping them?

Answer:
The current real estate market has created so many great bargains that it's literally impossible for any single company, no matter how big, to buy the entire available inventory. We already have a portfolio of properties and we have created an opportunity where everybody wins. You get a great deal on your investment that provides steady cash flow through the monthly income and significant long-term appreciation. The tenant-owner has an opportunity to buy the house from you down the road, thus fulfilling their desire to be homeowner. The community benefits with fewer vacant properties (vacant properties can drag down the value of an entire community).

Question:

Are you realtors?

Answer:

No, we are investors who are buying deeply discounted properties and rehabbing them and then placing tenants in the properties to provide you, the busy professional, with a turnkey investing solution.

Question:

What is the typical discount I am getting?

Answer:

Our properties are typically sold at 60% of the market value to rehabbers, 80% to 90% of the market value with a tenant already in place and all repairs fully completed to real estate investors who are interested in turn key properties.

"Believing in others is risky, but it can be the best decision you ever make in life" – *Rateb Rock Shukoor*

Bonus Section

Interviews with prominent investors by the author

Extraordinary
Results

by

Ordinary Investors

Golden nuggets from an experienced investor, Don DeRosa.

An Introduction to Don DeRosa

Don DeRosa is a real estate investor, author, teacher, coach and a national speaker. He was formerly the president of Georgia Real Estate Investors Association, one of the longest running REIAs in the country. Don has trained thousands of new and experienced investors to build wealth in real estate using the same techniques that helped him build his fortune, particularly by weaving ownership finance, private money, creatively structured deals and selling decisively. Honored among the top 21 real estate investors in the U.S. and

Canada, Don DeRosa was 'featured' in The New York Times best-selling book The Millionaire Real Estate Investor.

Don is the first Real Estate instructor in the country to move all of his course material, plus hundreds of hours of seminars, boot camps, video, and audio to the iPad in the iMasterReal Estate for the iPad series. Expanding his offerings to teach investors and agents on how to become Mobile Professionals Don DeRosa has included material on how to make more-work less, to be more efficient, productive and competitive. He has enveloped his entire knowledge of real estate and presented it with mobile technology on the iPad, iPhone, Android and other mobile devices.

Don DeRosa has bought and sold well over 250 properties in his investing career. This has given him the expertise and experience to train students on everything from sourcing owner's finance, purchase opportunities, negotiating successfully with sellers, analyzing deals, creating equity through short sales and making a substantial profit on every deal!

Don personally shares all of his inside secrets for generating both current cash flow and long-term wealth through his step-by-step real estate investing systems, both on the mobile devices and in hard copy, including:

- Building Wealth with Real Estate–The Ultimate Step-by-Step System For Creating a Top Real Estate Investment Business in Less Than 33 Days;

- Private Lending 101–The Ultimate Step by Step Guide to Utilizing Other People's Money;

- Sell Your House FAST for Maximum Profit – The Ultimate Step-by-Step Guide to Selling Your House Quickly in Any Market

- Expert Negotiating – Tools, Tactics and Strategies to Create Winning Deals

- He also trains via mobile devices on an ongoing project, for further details please check:

MobileRealEstateRockstar.com (for Investors), and

MobileRealEstateSuperstar.com (for Realtors) training sites

Through his detailed courses, CDs, blogs,

books, seminars, telecasts, online sites and personal mentoring and coaching, Don's students learn practical approaches to run "real" real estate investing businesses. He truly enjoys teaching and helping his students become financially independent, successful real estate entrepreneurs.

••

Rock: Hello, everyone how is everybody today, good I hope. We have a special guest here with us today Mr. Don DeRosa who was kind enough to allow us to conduct an interview with him on the current real estate industry. Mr. DeRosa has been in the real estate industry as an investor and educator for a long time and he is going to share some success strategies with us here today! Everybody I know who knows Mr. DeRosa has given me positive, not short from remarkable, feedback about his personal and professional stature. I have known Mr. DeRosa for a very long time as well and although I have not conducted any business with him being on different platforms, I have unprecedented respect for his accomplishments personally. Here he is, hello Don, how are you?

Don: I am very well, thank you Rock.

Rock: Instead of me going on and on about you Don, why don't you tell the audience a little about yourself!

Don: Well, I just said, my name is Don DeRosa. I live here in Johns Creek

Georgia, just north of Atlanta. I have been in this business since late 1997 and I started buying houses while I was working a full time job. Then I started teaching real estate in 2003 soon after which the GAREIA elected me as their president. I have done quite a few deals in my career. Real Estate is my passion. I have had my share of trials and error and of course, the paper clutter confusion from documents that causes undue stress. That is also the reason why we have come up with a training system for newbie realtors to do real estate completely paperless via mobile devices and applications.

Rock: Well, I actually listened to your

course. You did the iPad-seminar part 1 and then part 2. Each one was a good four hours of great information. That was in Atlanta REIA am I correct?

Don: Yes

Rock: I have listened to that and there is tons of good information on it. Guys, if you are thinking of getting any kind of mobile devices especially iPad, you need to really take Don's classes because he's showing you some stuff that you can't even imagine you can accomplish with an iPad or a mobile device.

Don: Yeah, Most people think that it is a toy or a big iPhone, but I will show you it is a whole lot more.

Rock: Oh yeah after I saw what you did with that, I knew there's a whole lot more to it than it seems. I actually have a Blackberry Playbook, which I am thinking about switching to iPad because of your classes. Tell me about your worst experience or worst deal.

Don: Well anybody that tells you that they have never lost money, do not believe them. –I can tell you I never lost money in a deal, but that is not true because on the very first renovation I did I bought from a wholesaler and they told me that it only needed a few thousand dollars, they also told me that the value was there! I got into it not knowing any better. Therefore, we started the contractor off on three-draw system, which I usually recommend. Half way through it, we ended up putting him on an hourly basis because he kept coming up with changes. "So let me just go on an hourly basis. It will be cheaper for you". Even then, I did not know better. What started as a $7500 renovation turned out to be over $40,000 in renovation. What was supposed to be a $30,000 profit turned into a huge deficit.

Rock: Okay

Don: And that was like the second or third house I ever did. That was my very first renovation. If you took a list of everything you could possibly do wrong on a renovation, I will check every one of them. However, I laugh about that when I think about it now.

Rock: Okay

Don: So the difference between a good deal and a bad deal in almost every case is time. You can take a bad deal and make it a good deal; you just have to have a lot of time. I joke about that and I tell that story a lot in my seminars. It was probably the worst experience but also the best experience because that gave me the experience- that was what you call a real life seminar.

Rock: An expensive one too

Don: Yes, that was an expensive seminar but man, I learned a lot from it. I learned a ton of what not to do. That was by far the best seminar that I ever went on because from that point onward I told myself "I'm not going down that path again" and I stick to my guns because I really understand how important it is to do so.

Rock: Don one thing I know is, many investors do not admit to losing money in a deal and they cannot tell you "Well I have never lost money in a deal". To my experience, if that is the answer it usually means two things. Either they are not telling you the truth or they have not done enough deals.

Don: That is what my experiences tell me as well.

Rock: Yeah

Don: Now, I will say this – for years I have not lost money.

Rock: Right

Don: Because of the system that I have put in and the stringent numbers that I used, I do not speculate.

Rock: Okay

Don: And I do not recommend anybody speculating. I mean people that are out of state like in the California markets, Florida markets; they may have an enormous amount of money to afford speculating on real estate…

Rock: Go on

Don: They buy something retail give it a few months, wait for the appreciation and then unload to make double digit profits. They make money hand over fist but the problem is if that market crashes, they lose everything.

Rock: Correct, you are right

Don: I mean anybody that tells you that they have not lost money on deals, just as you said earlier - A – they have not done enough deals or –B-they may not be telling you everything.

Rock: I totally agree.

Don: I mean this business allows you to make an awful lot of money, but you really need to know what you are doing. It is not hard. It is not rocket science, but you have to know what the criteria is involved and you have to stay within those limits. You do not want to be a motivated buyer.

Rock: Or seller.

Don: Or seller.

Rock: That is for sure.

Don: This is because when you become a motivated buyer and say "Okay. You are actually saying, I am a new investor. "I want to buy something" when you make that mistake and you just buy because you are anxious to buy, ultimately you will end up becoming a motivated seller.

Rock: Definitely, that is my experience too. I totally agree.

Don: That is right.

Rock: Now what did you learn from that deal? What I really believe in is that we learn from our good experiences but not as much as we learn from our bad experiences. They may be expensive seminars but they stick with you for the rest of your life.

Don: Absolutely, it is the best learning seminar I have ever been to. The biggest thing I have pulled out from it is, - never, ever, ever put your contractor on an hourly rate.

Rock: That is one.

Don: Okay trust but still verify everything.

Rock: Absolutely,

Don: Okay, there are all kinds of people out there in this world, some are truthful and outstanding and some are just out to make money. Sometimes you do not know the difference. Therefore, you have to take the information they give but do not trust what they say. Trust it but also verify it. Because I can go in and say – I can go with every deal, thinking everyone is being honest with me, but I also know from that experience, from that one experience I know that I trust but I still verify everything. I mean that is just what experience has taught me. I tell people "Trust is a great thing and you should trust everybody but you should also – you have a responsibility to yourself and everybody involved to verify the information that they have given you so that you can make sure".

Rock: I totally agree and it is just good business practice.

Don: That is the two biggest things I learned.

Rock: I totally agree. Not trusting anything or anybody is not the way to live, yet again trusting yet verifying is the best thing to do in business, especially in real estate deals. As you said you did not know the person that was selling the property to you, how honest they were being with you and how truthful they were about the numbers, the deal or any other information they were sharing.

Don: I mean there are many good wholesalers out there. I just happen to get the one that I guess was 'monetarily challenged'– they thought money was more important than their integrity.

Rock: Yeah

Don: It was a good lesson for me to learn.

Rock: Okay Well…

Rock: And you made money after that because of those lessons you learned from that one bad deal.

Don: I make more money at the bad deals because of the bad deals than I do because of the good deals.

Rock: I know exactly what you mean Don. For now, I would like to thank you Don, for being here with us today sharing your experiences. Thank You Don!

Don: Thank you Rock for having me

Rock: It was a pleasure.

Notes:

_____

_____

_____

Some info about Rock's services

Special Offer Free 16 minute CD

Do you have any investments or any capital that is not getting you double digits return on you investment, safely and is secured by a solid asset?

If yes, I now have a program that will pay you 20 times more in returns than you can probably get anywhere else. (NO, it's not MLM)

I have a 16 minutes CD that explains my program. Contact me if you would like it for free.

678-318-1888

www.RockTheInvestor@gmail.com

No obligation and I guarantee that your 16 minutes will be well spent.

Special $297 Offer For FREE

(Only For Readers of This Book)

Have you decided to be successful in real estate investing NOW?

Success Coaching, A Plan of Action to Freedom Through Real Estate
"A personalized coaching program that works"
By Rock Shukoor, the results coach!

I am starting a very goal oriented and systematic series of coaching sessions for my new coaching clients!

Below are short lists of action items you can plan for by working with me:

* Plan for each meeting to be one hour, 30 minutes of that is education or a case study and the other 30 minutes will be Q & A.
* Plan on having us as your accountability partner, we keep track of the results
* Plan on learning exciting and new ways of closing deals
* Plan on becoming a success.
* Plan to close deals or more deals without using your own money or credit
* Plan on working with me as I am dedicated to your success
* Plan to implement the action plan we provide you
* Plan on taking action, that is the only thing you need to do with the information I will share with you, take action!

678-318-1888

www.RockTheInvestor@gmail.com

www.HasselfreeREMentorship.com

Call and schedule a complementary, 30 minutes No obligation consulting for FREE. (Valued at $297)

My way of saying, thank you for believing in me and taking your time to read my book.

Pearls from an experienced investor, Joe Thompson

An Introduction to Joe Thompson

Joe Thompson is an experienced business and financial consultant with over 40 years of experience, consulting and business ownership dating back to 1970. Joe entered the financial consulting field in 1982 and has since received numerous awards for his achievements and quality of service. Joe's practice focuses primarily on working with Real Estate Investors, Entrepreneurs and Business Owners, all of whom present unique challenges and opportunities, which require experience, expertise and additional skills not commonly found in the advisement industry. He has been an owner or equity partner in 19 different businesses ranging from retailing to consulting and from start up to reorganization. Joe's real estate investing career however, began 11 years ago and it includes 2 years as a full time investor. Joe is currently involved in five different ventures two of which produce passive incomes.

As a board member and advisor for many companies, Joe is exceptionally well qualified to train and consult on many areas of business and personal finances.

Joe Thomson is currently a sub group leader for Atlanta REIA and North Metro REIA and is on the speakers list for both of these organizations as well as others. Joe is also the founder and leader of Haves and Wants

Atlanta's premier networking meeting for Real Estate Investors having produced over $129,000,000 in transactions over its 7-year history. Last year Haves & Wants had 1,678 attendees with closings of over $19,000,000.

Joe Thompson's 'A Good Deal'

Rock: Hi Joe, How are you?
Joe: Hi, I am doing fine Rock, how are you this evening?

Rock: I'm doing wonderful. Thank you. I have known you for quite a while Joe. Tell us, how long have you done real estate?

Joe: I have been doing real estate for 11 or 12 years now.

Rock: Okay, I know you have seen many good things and some of the not so good things and some stuff that we have lost money on. 'And' if you have not lost any money in some of the real estate deals, you really are not doing real estate deals. Tell us Joe, about the best deals that you have done in realty.

Joe: Okay In discussing this with you earlier and looking at it, I actually came upon something that I had truly forgotten and it was my first mobile home deal.

Rock: Okay, please continue

Joe: It was outside Cincinnati, Ohio and it was an incredible deal. I was not interested in mobile homes in any way at first. I didn't want to hear about it, I had no interest in it, it just wasn't something I'd ever consider until a friend of mine who was my partner in the deal showed me the numbers. And what we did is we bought a 167-pad mobile home park at 87% occupancy, no rentals, all purchased homes and we only had the money out of our pockets to purchase for 45 days. We got our money back because we packaged and sold the notes on all the homes, which paid for our purchase price of the park and we were cash flow positive from that point forward on the deal. Now, for the last close to seven years, I have been receiving quarterly checks on disbursements from this deal and I get them every quarter, four times a year.

Rock: Wow that sounds good: So how much of your own time did it take to put the deal together?

Joe: My time was not bad because I had a partner in the deal. I was the 'money guy', had the knowledge, get the numbers, and cast the notes. I had maybe three or four hours in it. I did have some capital outlay for 45 days, but two of the primary questions I asked, one: do I have to go to Cincinnati, Ohio? The answer was no. And two, do I ever have to knock on someone's door going "Excuse me. You owe me your payment for last month". The answer there also was no. Then we looked at the cash controls once I was comfortable with them and the management. How can you not go into a deal where your money is only out of your pocket for 45 days?

Rock: All right and you get a great upside.

Joe: Oh, yes. Well the upside really is not so great because it's mobile homes, so there will be no appreciation.

Rock: Right, but you get the cash flow.

Joe: The cash flow is incredible.

Rock: Yes

Joe: And I am still getting 30% of the cash flow. Like I said this is six or seven years ago. We have no issues. When somebody leaves, they do not take their mobile home with them.

Rock: Yes, that is true

Joe: You send them a removal order to take their property off your land or sign the title. They sign the title and send it back. We resell them and every time we have five notes that we are carrying we have a secondary market that takes our notes.

Rock: That sounds great man. So it didn't take any of your own time, your money was in it for 45 days and you have been getting cash flow for the last six or seven years from the deal that you did.

Joe: That is correct.

Rock: And you did not have to travel all the way to Cincinnati. You do not do that at all. You are not dealing with tenants, with their toilets, termites, none of that.

Joe: At this point, I am passive only.

Rock: You sure are, it seems!

Joe: And one thing I like about the sale of mobile homes as opposed to the rentals, if they need a plumber, our guy onsite refers them to a plumber because it is their mobile home.

Rock: Right, that sounds good. Now tell me about your worst deals and the deal that you…Before we go there, if you do not mind, how much money did you make at the beginning of that if you want to share that?

Joe: On that one when we sold the notes after we recast the long-term debt with a ten-year commercial note on the property we made about $55,000 each.

Rock: Okay, and there are two partners.

Joe: Correct.

Rock: Okay, great

Joe Thompson Bad Deal

Rock: All right, so tell me about one of your worst deals and a deal that you lost some money or time on.

Joe: Well fortunately, I am actually one of those who have not lost money.

Rock: Okay

Joe: But my worst deal is a group of homes that I bought where I did not actually go out and prove my rental rates myself. I bought these three houses as a group in a market that is not one of the better markets. And I missed the rental rates and I missed it significantly. Instead of receiving a check without looking every quarter, I compelled to write three checks instead every quarter.

Rock: Whoa, okay

Joe: I actually still at this point – that part of my career where I hired management and yet I had to deal with tenant issues. I was taking calls late at night that this or the other this is not working. I hated it. To add to my woe I had to write checks out each month. The good news is I was able to sell them tenanted and make a small profit under $2000 each after holding them for six months.

Rock: A clever move, so what did you learn from your worst deal? We usually learn a lot more from our bad deals than we learn from our good deals, isn't that a fact?

Joe: Well my learning on that one is something we all should know. Many of us who has learned forget and sometimes we need to 'be reminded' of the same lesson occasionally: do your own due diligence. Make sure you know what your numbers are because guess what? They are your numbers. They are not the guy who said this is what the rentals are in this market. That is my money; I need to know my numbers and I do not need to trust somebody else for my numbers without confirmation.

Rock: Okay, all right the big lesson there was to do your due diligence and be diligent about them.

Joe: Be diligent with your due diligence.

Rock: Yes okay

Joe Thompson Advice

Rock: You have done real estate for over ten years now and everyone, what would your advice be to new real estate investors?

Joe: Probably the number one thing in addition to education is to look at people and find people who are actually doing real estate and doing the type of real estate you want to do. Probably the single biggest detriment I see that somebody actually starting out is they look at all the different trainings, they go through a ton of 'trainings' and they get very confused and they have trouble picking a concept. Do I want to do subject two's? Do I want a buy on the courthouse? How do they want to buy? Pick a technique, learn it, and master that technique when it is making you money then look to expand into other types of real estate and other techniques. There is no one best deal. If there is one best, way to make money in real estate everybody will be doing it and nobody will be making any money at it.

Rock: Okay that sounds great. I am sure you have read the book Good to Great, right.

Joe: Oh, yes.

Rock: That is what you are advising them – to learn what you really are good at, become a master at that and then learn other things. You need to be excellent at least in one thing.

Joe: Correct and it is not just real estate. In most endeavors in commerce, the hugely successful people are myopic. They do one thing incredibly well. Those are the hugely successful people. Steve Jobs with Apple, Gates with Microsoft, Warren Buffet, even Donald Trump, they do one thing and they do one thing very well.

Generally, when they get out of that one thing they lose the use of their core competencies, they have some amount of hubris and thinking they can do something well just because they did something else well and that is not necessarily true.

Rock: I totally agree with you. Look at Michael Jordan.

Joe: Oh, yeah

Rock: The greatest basketball player

Joe: But not much of the golfer

Rock: Or baseball player.

Joe: thank you so much for the great information you have shared with us. I appreciate the time and trouble you have taken for being with us here today and I look forward to hearing

about your future profitable deals and
accomplishments.

Notes:

_____

_____

_____

_____

Some info about Rock's services

Special Offer Free 16 minute CD

Do you have any investments or any capital that is not getting you double digits return on you investment, safely and is secured by a solid asset?

If yes, I now have a program that will pay you 20 times more in returns than you can probably get anywhere else. (NO, it's not MLM)

I have a 16 minutes CD that explains my program. Contact me if you would like it for free.

678-318-1888

www.RockTheInvestor@gmail.com

No obligation and I guarantee that your 16 minutes will be well spent.

Special $297 Offer For FREE

(Only For Readers of This Book)

Have you decided to be successful in real estate investing NOW?

Success Coaching, A Plan of Action to Freedom Through Real Estate
"A personalized coaching program that works"

By Rock Shukoor, the results coach!

I am starting a very goal oriented and systematic series of coaching sessions for my new coaching clients!

Below are short lists of action items you can plan for by working with me:

* Plan for each meeting to be one hour, 30 minutes of that is education or a case study and the other 30 minutes will be Q & A.
* Plan on having us as your accountability partner, we keep track of the results
* Plan on learning exciting and new ways of closing deals
* Plan on becoming a success.
* Plan to close deals or more deals without using your own money or credit
* Plan on working with me as I am dedicated to your success
* Plan to implement the action plan we provide you
* Plan on taking action, that is the only thing you need to do with the information I will share with you, take action!

678-318-1888

www.RockTheInvestor@gmail.com

www.HasselfreeREMentorship.com

Call and schedule a complementary, 30 minutes No obligation consulting for FREE. (Valued at $297)

My way of saying, thank you for believing in me and taking your time to read my book.

We Buy Houses
$CASH$
ANY CONDITION, ANY SITUATION, ANY AREA, ANY PRICE

Do you own an unwanted house and need to sell quickly? Are you in Foreclosure? Are you behind on Payments? Is your house Vacant? Need Repairs? Relocating? Divorce, Bad Tenant? Owe Liens? 100% Financed? Estate Sale or Fire Damage?

Is your house upside down? We can help!

Call me NOW and ask for a free report 'How to sell your house in 10 days"
Visit us at
www.WeBuyHousesCashNow.com

Or CALL NOW

(404) 419-6222

Rubies from an experienced investor, Steve Jordan

A Biography

Born 1935 in Bucharest, Romania, lived in Bulgaria, then immigrated to USA in 1940 and grew up in Kenmore, NY, a suburb of Buffalo. Steve was student body president in high school and graduated with a political science major from Penn State in 1957. He was also a member of Sigma Alpha Epsilon fraternity, president in senior year. He was 'commissioned' as an Ensign into US Navy upon graduation. Served in both Atlantic and Pacific fleets between 1957 and 1960.

Worked for IBM Corporation from 1960 to 1991, rising from computer salesman to senior management positions in the Atlanta division headquarters. Upon retirement from IBM, he turned his attention to real estate investing, which he started in as a part time business in 1975. Since 1991, he has purchased, rehabbed and re-sold over 75 houses while building a portfolio of 35 rental units. He now retains over 15 rental units, which he manages.

Steve Jordan's Good Deal

Rock: Steve, if you can tell me about your best deals that you have done, describe them a little for us.

Steve: Well, my best deal is probably a house that I bought down in the Grant Park area. It is a house that I really did not ever want to buy. I used to advertise that I buy houses and I used to get a lot of phone calls. One day, a woman called me and said she had a house for sale and gave me the address. I told her that I will go look at it and I did. She was such a good seller. She had just put the key under the doormat and let anybody that she talked to into the house. I looked at the house and it was an old three bedroom, one bathhouse with only a wall furnace, not even a central heat. Moreover, when I got back to my office, I called her back and said, "Gee, I'm sorry. I'm not interested." she replied, "Mr. Jordan, you have to buy my house.

My husband told me to make the house disappear." Well if there is a good definition of a motivated seller, she was obviously a motivated seller. When we all came to the detail about why her husband said to make the house disappear, it turned out that she had a very small loan on the property. She was willing to let me take it over subject to the loan. I did some very basic paint and carpet fix up and quickly rented it out. I was getting about $350, $400 a month positive cash flow. I had several tenants in it over the next five or six years. Eventually I decided to 'take a look' at the house after such a long time and to my amazement Grant Park area had come up substantially in the intervening period of time. From there, I decided to make a significant investment in that house. I gutted it and I enclosed the car porch, made a master bedroom suite, and added a brand new kitchen. On top of that, I added central heat, air-conditioning and all the trimmings. I re-landscaped it. I did literally everything that you would want to do. After which, I put it out in the market. I sold that house within 60 days. When all the smoke cleared and I paid off the loan and paid back my fix up costs and all of that, I walked away with just under

$100,000 net, net, net, net profit. I guess that does not even include the positive cash flow I had in the years that I had it as a rental property.

So for a house that I did not want to buy and the woman talked me into it, it turned out to be an extremely profitable transaction. The best part of the situation was when I got the house all finished and refurbished, I went back and talked to the woman from whom I bought the house from and said would you like to see what I have done to it, she said, "Yeah." I picked her up at her office one day and we drove down there. I let her walk through the house and instead of being mad at me for doing all the good work and now making a significant profit in the house, there were tears in her eyes. Her reason for it was "you've made this house everything that I ever wanted it to be and I'm so happy that somebody now will get to enjoy it".

Thank you for showing me how nice the house turned out in the end. And so it warms your heart when I was able help the lady make the house disappear because her husband was tired of having to go fix it up between the bad tenants that they put in it and then having her see what the house's real potential was. It brought a big smile to her face and tears to her eyes. It almost made me choke up at that time. Even thinking about it has that choking effect on me.

Rock: Okay, to recap that, you purchased the property subject to a loan, which means you just took over her mortgage...

Steve: I just took over her existing loan. I did not give her any money at all.

Rock: So no money at all, you fixed up the property to some basic stuff, not really a high investment.

Steve: Just paint and carpet

Rock: Yes, paint and carpet.

Steve: It cost me about $3,000.

Rock: Okay, so you are in it for 'basically just $3,000?'

Steve: Uh huh

Rock: Okay and then you found – you rented the property for a very long time and got a positive cash flow out of it.

Steve: I got positive cash flow for about five or six years.

Rock: Okay and then you sold the property when the market had shifted. That time, the values of the houses in that area had gone up therefore you had lots of equity so you sold the property for about $100,000 of profit.

Steve: Indeed

Rock: After all expenses paid of that was for one single family home the 'small deal' paid of big returns in other words.

Steve: Well the return was almost infinite because I had almost no capital in it.

Rock: That is one thing, you did not use a lot of your time, right, because someone else did the rehab for you?

Steve: Yeah, I hired out the rehab, but in almost all the rehabs that I did and I have rehabbed probably well over 75 houses, I don't want to say I was hands on because I didn't do any of the work, but I was very fortunate my wife is professionally trained as an architect. She owned her own interior decorating business at one time. Every time I went in and did anything significant in rehabbing a house, the first person I would bring in would be my wife. We would develop all the rehab details together.

Rock: That is where a good partner comes in play, right?

Steve: Absolutely

Rock: Okay, in your case, your partner is your wife as well as your life partner to.

Steve: Absolutely, yes

Rock: Okay, great

Steve Jordan Bad Deal

Rock: Now I am sure, for as long as you have done real estate, you have some experience of doing some deals that you are not very happy with, so tell me about one of those, bad deals.

Steve: You are going to embarrass me.

Rock: We could learn a lot from there. So, that is okay.

Steve: I will embarrass myself.

Rock: And if we have not done any bad real estate deals, we are not investing at all.

Steve: Well, that means that you have – it is a good way to put it. You have not done very much or else you are lying.

Rock: Right

Steve: The worst thing that ever happened to me in real estate is back in the

80's. It was quite a while ago. I invested in an apartment complex. Somebody had bought the apartment complex and had divided it up. They sold the buildings off, as 'quadruplexes', and I bought a building that was eight units. I bought the equivalent of two quadruplexes. Many other investors bought the other buildings the same way as I did. We had a real estate broker, professional real estate broker, licensed broker who was our property manager. He did the screening of the tenants, collected the rents, paid the bills and he maintained the pool and the wash up dryer facilities, etc., etc. It was quite a large complex, about 200 total units. I had the misfortune or fortune of being 'elected' President of the owners group that oversaw the broker. Everything went along fine for about two or three years until one day, the property manager called me up and said, "Steve, I've got a problem. Come on down. I've got to talk to you." I went down there and sat down with him. I will not use his name, but what he had basically done was he had pooled our money with that of another apartment complex. That apartment complex was not nearly as successful as ours was so he had drained all of our money into this other apartment complex. At that point where he could not pay to have the grass cut, the water bill, which was a common water bill, etc. Eventually we all let our units go into foreclosure because as the situation got worse and worse, our other owners took their units out of the rental pool and were collecting the rent themselves. There was less and less money coming in to the property manager and the whole thing slid downhill. Every owner in there eventually went to foreclosure. I guess the lesson, the biggest lesson I learned was that you needed to be in control. I did not have control. None of the other owners had control. We put our faith and confidence in a licensed broker who had some legal requirements in Georgia law that he did not pay attention to and it let us all go right down the tube. I vowed that based on that experience 'to never ever again let anyone else be in control of the property or the money'. Although I did many partnerships after that, the partnerships were always with me being in control.

Rock: Okay, one thing I have learned is, in order to have a successful business; you must know your numbers at all times and be in control of your money. Even when you have a property manager, you must be in control of the money.

Steve: And if the other person was, there for learning experience. I would have control of the cash flow, the investment and the rehab, etc. So, don't ever let yourself lose control of the situation because then, you're counting on people who may not have the ethics, honesty and good will that hopefully you have as an individual.

Rock: That is a good lesson to learn Steve. I can vouch further that you have done very well for yourself and your partners because in the last eleven years that I have been around Georgia REIA and other investors that know you and I know them so obviously no one has ever talked bad about you or said anything negative about you. It is also the reason as to why I am interviewing you.

Steve: Oh, that is nice to hear.

Rock: Yeah that is a good thing. As far as being in real estate is concerned, your reputation speaks very highly of you. It can take you a very long time to build it and allows you to be successful or close 'a lot' of deals.

Steve: Well, I appreciate that. Thank you.

Rock: All right so from that lesson, from that deal you learned not to let anyone be in control. For you to be in control you would really need to know what is going on.

Steve: Yes, you do and I think that for everybody reading this book, they should take it a step further. I will give you an example of what I mean.

Back when I was a hard moneylender, I often was asked to lend, for example, on a duplex and I would go look at the property and look at the surrounding property. Many times, it was a dead end street with all duplexes. I tried to explain to the potential investor that he would not or she would not be in control because the rental value of his or her duplex would depend on what the other owners of the duplexes on that street would do, how well they maintain their property, what kind of tenants they choose. He or she 'will be covered' by what the other owners on that street did. And it's something that – because I learned the bad lesson or a very strong lesson financially, I tried to make sure that other people didn't have the same bad experience that I have and not understand what control really means.

I know that when you buy, for example, a single-family house, you certainly do not control what your neighbors do, but most single-family homeowners want the same the thing that you do and that is for their home to appreciate, too look good, they have pride in their neighborhood, etc. Therefore, you really do not have the problem when you are 'surrounded' by single-family residences that are predominantly owned by residents, owner occupied. Therefore, I know you cannot have 100% control in that situation, but you generally do not have the problem that one would have with duplexes or triplexes.

It is that kind of control that I think is very important. Think through how I could lose control and if there is a way, then 'maybe' that is not a good investment that you want to participate in.

Rock: Okay, great. Well, that is a great lesson to learn, expensive lesson from one deal, a very expensive lesson, but unless we do deals and multiple deals, otherwise we will not learn what we should not be doing. Now the good thing is you can learn from other people their mistakes and experiences and that is what will help us in the future.

Steve: And not repeat the mistakes that people like me have made.

Rock: Yes, do the right things and make sure do not follow the same steps especially in a bad deal like that. Do not repeat that. So be in control and learn from people like you, Mr. Jordan.

Steve Jordan Advice

Rock: Having 35 to 40 years' experience in real estate, what advice would you give an investor or a new investor?

Steve: I would say the best thing to do is get a lot of education. As I said at the beginning of this interview with the first investment property I bought, it was a 16-unit apartment house. In addition, I bought that based on what I read in a less than 100 page book that I picked up in the bookstore. That is not a good situation to start with.

I would suggest that people learn from other experienced real estate investors through their REIA or other avenues. Not just from books but from real life people who have a record of accomplishment and know what they are doing, have a reputation for success and honesty and integrity. Moreover, those kind of people that will set you in the right direction and they will be able to give some good advice on what to do and not to do and how to accomplish what your own goals are.

You need to sit down and really think through what your personal objectives and goals are so that you know where you are going and not just bounce around like a pinball inside a pinball game.

Rock: That is great advice. I totally agree with you. Well Steve, thank you very much for your time, I am sure we will talk again.

Steve: My pleasure, thank you.

Notes:

_____

_____

_____

Some info about Rock's services

Special Offer Free 16 minute CD

Do you have any investments or any capital that is not getting you double digits return on you investment, safely and is secured by a solid asset?

If yes, I now have a program that will pay you 20 times more in returns than you can probably get anywhere else. (NO, it's not MLM)

I have a 16 minutes CD that explains my program. Contact me if you would like it for free.

678-318-1888

www.RockTheInvestor@gmail.com

No obligation and I guarantee that your 16 minutes will be well spent.

Special $297 Offer For FREE

(Only For Readers of This Book)

Have you decided to be successful in real estate investing NOW?

Success Coaching, A Plan of Action to Freedom Through Real Estate
"A personalized coaching program that works"
By Rock Shukoor, the results coach!

I am starting a very goal oriented and systematic series of coaching sessions for my new coaching clients!

Below are short lists of action items you can plan for by working with me:

* Plan for each meeting to be one hour, 30 minutes of that is education or a case study and the other 30 minutes will be Q & A.
* Plan on having us as your accountability partner, we keep track of the results
* Plan on learning exciting and new ways of closing deals
* Plan on becoming a success.
* Plan to close deals or more deals without using your own money or credit
* Plan on working with me as I am dedicated to your success
* Plan to implement the action plan we provide you
* Plan on taking action, that is the only thing you need to do with the information I will share with you, take action!

678-318-1888

www.RockTheInvestor@gmail.com

www.HasselfreeREMentorship.com

Call and schedule a complementary, 30 minutes No obligation consulting for FREE. (Valued at $297)

My way of saying, thank you for believing in me and taking your time to read my book.

Diamonds from an experienced investor, Steve Brown

Short Biography:

Steve has an MBA in Finance & Marketing. He is a General Contractor, Licensed Residential & Commercial Real Estate Broker, Certified Tax Preparer, Real Estate Tax Consultant, Member of the Association Georgia Real Estate Exchange Group. Besides being an apartment consultant, Educator of Cash Cows Commercial Real Estate Group under Atlanta REIA, He is also a Spec Builder in Dunwoody, Brookhaven. Steve Brown is a High End Rehabber in the Emory area sold to Doctors, Attorneys, & IT people. He is also a builder of shopping centers, AAAA GAS, convenience stores & fast food restaurants, among others. He has also developed several subdivisions and built & sold self-storage units and still owns part of an Assisted Living facility. He owned several businesses including Atlanta Archery & Gun Range, Your Serve sandwich shop, GEM tank less water Heater Company with patent & UL approval, five video stores, and a pizza and sub-shop. He is also a hotel consultant for the Sheraton.

Steve Brown, Good Deal

Rock: Hi, we have Steve Brown here with us today and Steve has over 30 years of experience in the property investment market. Is that correct Steve?

Steve: Yes Rock, that is correct.

Rock: He is an expert in single-family homes as well as commercial properties. Steve, if you can tell us about your best real estate deal, pertaining to the details of that deal

Steve: It was a two-story traditional house located in the country on five acres of land.

Rock: Wow, how much money did you make out of that deal?

Steve: $80,000

Rock: $80,000, that is excellent! How long did it take you to do it?

Steve: It took me a year.

Rock: One year, all right, what kind of resources did you use? Tell us about the deal itself and then about the resources that you utilized.

Steve: Okay, do you want me to give you specifics of how I started? I was not a rehabber to begin with. I was a new homebuilder.

Rock: Okay, please continue

Steve: Well, building new homes is a little different. I was not a custom homebuilder, but I had a stock of three homes at a total probably of a million and a half and I had to figure out how to sell them. Therefore, I took a course that taught you how to do it, what you learn from it are buy wholesale – and the methods of doing it. I instantly picked up on the subject. I learned that one of the best ways to advertise was these signs, the yellow signs with the black writing on them. And of course, I cannot write well, so I used this method as my primary way of selling my homes. I succeeded in doing that right before the crash really took a big effect.

The other thing that I did was, I put a lease with an option to buy on this particular house in Jefferson in Jackson County. Normally I would not go out that far because I was working, but it looked like a good deal and I decided to meet the person, the house needed no repairs, except for what I saw on the front plus some landscaping. A big house in a good area, I looked at it and then went to Real Quest for information and found out that I could probably get, in a good day, $250,000 to $260,000 for it.

I went to her and I said "Okay. You owe this much", knowing all the 'facts' which, I got from the course. As part of the course, we got access to a guy that was providing us with the leads which they had a side deal with the instructor. I capitalized on that and they were just great about everything. 30 days later, I had my first deal. I was talking to this woman and she says, "I have diabetes, I am overweight, I can't get a job. I need to get out of my house.

My son has a house that I want to move into and needs about $40,000". She did not give me the exact amount but somewhere around that to rehab the basement where she can live in. I said "Okay".

So in every one of these deals something strange comes up all the time. I mean I was just going to freak out but I said "Okay". Here is the deal. I will take your mortgage and I will give you enough money to move from here to your son's, which is only half a mile away. It was plain luck. You have good luck and bad luck in these things.

What I did was negotiate the deal and I said "Okay. What am I going to get? $45,000 on this house" plus the $160,000 and add the $5000 on closing. That was it. I said "Okay. I'm going to do a lease option". Before I even closed on this, I stuck my corny sign out there on a street that I figured nobody was driving on. I mean it was a highway between one of the roads that goes up to Athens – in North Georgia – and right back into the city of Jefferson. I said, "Nobody goes on this road. What am I doing?" I put that sign up and I had five calls the first week – mostly tire-kickers. The second week went by three tire kickers. I said, "This is good. At least I got somebody calling on the sides".

This went on for about six weeks and I was going to close because it was near Christmas time. She did not want to close. I had a contract written October. She wants to close in January. I said "Thank you". In the meantime, I was looking for $45,000 and I came up with the funds through a private moneylender. He was a friend of mine. What happened was I got into the house and she was so fussy about it. It was unreal. She was also a paralegal – another problem. I mean these things come up all the time. You just have to persevere and have fun and go after it. That is my game plan.

Therefore, what I did, I said, "all right here's what it is". As soon as I got halfway down the rehab, I had a bite for a lease option from a young woman that ran a trucking company. Plenty of money, I had checked her out. She said, "I want to move in a bigger house" and I said "Fine. I've got exactly what you want".

The deal 'was done' on a lease option. As I 'was told' to mark the price up on a lease option, I figured the appraisal would be about $250,000. I marked it up to $290,000. I said "Uh-oh! Time is good for me. Maybe the appraisal will go up". Well of course, the market was going down. It appraised at $285,000. I made about $80,000 clear.

Rock: So you bought the property for $160,000. You gave the woman $45,000. You rehabbed the property and then you sold it for $285,000.

Steve: Yeah

Rock: Okay and it took you about one year to do that.

Steve: It did not take that long 'to actually do' the rehab and the other stuff, but the waiting time...

Rock: Hmm, the waiting time

Steve: For them to close, they were supposed to close before then.

Rock: Okay

Steve: But I was still afraid of the appraisal.

Rock: Yeah

Steve: And in writing the contracts, which are very difficult. You need to put in a clause in there so you 'are not caught blindsided'.

Rock: I agree

Steve: If the appraisal was going down, I was going out with less money or no money so that is an important issue that I was 'really concerned' about. I re-wrote the subject to contracts myself...

Rock: And?

Steve: But I did not know enough to put that in there. I knew what the law was on how much you could take, I got $16,000 from here...

Rock: Okay

Steve: From the lease option, that is.

Rock: Hmmm...

Steve: After that, I got a writ. I think her payment was $1,000. I got $3,000 a month so I was making $2,000 a month.

Rock: Out of the $1,000

Steve: But I had $45,000 pay back to my friend.

Rock: Let me clarify that. You said you found the money from a private lender. Therefore, you did not have any of your own money in the deal.

Steve: Not one dime

Rock: And then when you found the new buyer – so you bought the property with no money out of your pocket. You used someone else's money to buy it. Then when you found a buyer for the property, which was the lease option buyer, you collected $16,000 at the beginning and an additional $2,000 after that for one year?

Steve: That is correct.

Rock: Okay, all right. That is a great deal. But how much of your personal time was involved in that?

Steve: Very little

Rock: Maybe a few hours

Steve: The rehab, I sent a person out there to fix the gutter in the roof.

Rock: Wonderful.

Steve: That was it on the rehab. Then I sent a couple my people to work for me because I was still in the building business. I was just hanging on by my threads to get rid of these. I had contracts on all of them but I also had an overhead that was going out that was on the reel that I had to cover. Time wise, I spent it on going out there and putting the sign up and another few trips to make sure the sign was still up.

Rock: Remarkable!

Steve: Answering the phone was the other thing. That was it.

Rock: So I would say a maximum of ten hours of your own time. Or by the time you found it, you negotiated the deal, you put signs in there, you answered some phone calls, you took care of the documents and have to sign it and then you found a buyer and sign the documents with her and from there on that's it.

Steve: That was it.

Rock: So basically, you made your money not by working hard but by working smart and let your knowledge work for you.

Steve: Exactly, exactly.

Rock: All right wonderful, $80,000 is a lot of money out of one deal.

Steve: On the first deal on that title transaction.

Rock: Yeah.

Rock: Tell me about your worst deal. What did you do and how much did you lose on your worst deal?

Steve: I really did not lose that much, but I learned a lot and it was about 30 years ago, okay?

Rock: Okay.

Steve Brown, Bad Deal Lesson

Rock: So what was the lesson you learned from that deal?

Steve: Well, two things do your due diligence better than what I did. Just because you think you got a deal you may not have one. There are certain things like owners, titles if you do not get it, which taught me a lesson. I had another house I bought a long time ago, maybe 15 years ago, that I got the owner's title on because of this transaction. There was a – I think the pipeline running underneath the house or right beside it. It was eight feet for a water line from the water department...

Rock: Yeah...

Steve: Across the property, I had to collect on my owner's title to get my money back. I was lucky. I insured the land and the house when I found out that I had that problem.

Rock: I would say based on that experience, the lessons that you learned is one: to do better due diligence.

Steve: Right

Rock: And the second thing is, if you are buying a property, get insurance.

Steve: Right

Rock: And title insurance, mostly.

Steve: Yeah and I made a mistake of not using a closing attorney.

Rock: Okay.

Steve: That was my third one.

Rock: You have tons of experience with real estate. What would be your advice to a new investor or to any investor, what would be your best – golden nugget that you can give away?

Steve: That is a good question. The one thing I would say is that everybody is getting educated into what you are doing. Each education is the same to a certain degree, but each thing that you learn; you need to pick out the best thing out of them if you do several courses, which many people do. You need to find the niche, which is the hardest thing to do. What am I going to do? Buy, wholesale, rehab and wholesale and how do I find the leads and how do I sell the thing? These are 'the things' that you need to 'concentrate on', no matter what. I know I am not totally in the internet marketing deal today, but that is where I believe we are and that is where everything comes from. That is it.

Rock: That is a great advice thank you Steve and thank you for your time.

Some info about Rock's services

Special Offer Free 16 minute CD

Do you have any investments or any capital that is not getting you double digits return on you investment, safely and is secured by a solid asset?

If yes, I now have a program that will pay you 20 times more in returns than you can probably get anywhere else. (NO, it's not MLM)

I have a 16 minutes CD that explains my program. Contact me if you would like it for free.

678-318-1888

www.RockTheInvestor@gmail.com

No obligation and I guarantee that your 16 minutes will be well spent.

Special $297 Offer For FREE

(Only For Readers of This Book)

Have you decided to be successful in real estate investing NOW?

Success Coaching, A Plan of Action to Freedom Through Real Estate
"A personalized coaching program that works"
By Rock Shukoor, the results coach!

I am starting a very goal oriented and systematic series of coaching sessions for my new coaching clients!

Below are short lists of action items you can plan for by working with me:

* Plan for each meeting to be one hour, 30 minutes of that is education or a case study and the other 30 minutes will be Q & A.
* Plan on having us as your accountability partner, we keep track of the results
* Plan on learning exciting and new ways of closing deals
* Plan on becoming a success.
* Plan to close deals or more deals without using your own money or credit
* Plan on working with me as I am dedicated to your success
* Plan to implement the action plan we provide you
* Plan on taking action, that is the only thing you need to do with the information I will share with you, take action!

678-318-1888

www.RockTheInvestor@gmail.com

www.HasselfreeREMentorship.com

Call and schedule a complementary, 30 minutes No obligation consulting for FREE. (Valued at $297)

My way of saying, thank you for believing in me and taking your time to read my book.

We Buy Houses
$CASH$
ANY CONDITION, ANY SITUATION, ANY AREA, ANY PRICE

Do you own an unwanted house and need to sell quickly? Are you in Foreclosure? Are you behind on Payments? Is your house Vacant? Need Repairs? Relocating? Divorce, Bad Tenant? Owe Liens? 100% Financed? Estate Sale or Fire Damage?

Is your house upside down? We can help!

Call me NOW and ask for a free report 'How to sell your house in 10 days"

Visit us at

www.WeBuyHousesCashNow.com

Or CALL NOW

(404) 419-6222

Emeralds from an experience investor, Chris Littleton

Chris Littleton, Introduction

I spent 21 years in the airline industry and was tired of working in the corporate world and was looking for a way out. I attended a meeting on real estate investing in early 2002, purchased some real estate investment education to help me understand what I was getting into and I have not stopped learning about real estate from that day on. The best way to become successful in real estate investing is thru education, never stop learning, network with the people who are doing it right to see what really works in the market place and find you a good mentor. I was blessed to have found good education, a good network of investors and a great mentor to advise me and move me down the right path to success. Now I find no greater pleasure than to give back to those who wish to start their path to real estate investing and financial freedom. I wish the best of business to all who dream the dream!

Chris Littleton, President of Georgia Real Estate Investors Association for 2012-2013

Chris Littleton with his wife Donna own Solutions Realty Network, Inc. (SRNhomes.com) a full service property management brokerage. They share a passion for seeking out sound real estate investment opportunities. Their commitment to making investment properties profitable is realized through standardized renovations, reliable property management, and consistent maintenance. The team at Solutions Realty Network prides itself on being the experts in the property management field and proves it by successfully managing nearly 600 single Family homes & multifamily properties in 17 metro Atlanta counties.

Chris has been an active real estate investor and property manager since 2003. He and his companies have assisted investors worldwide at acquiring well over $110 Million of Investment Property in just a few years. He and his team also keep those investment properties preforming at the highest level of returns in their market place. Chris is a member of the National Association of Realtors (NAR), the National Association of Residential Property Managers (NARPM), a Certified International Immigration & Investment Specialist in the field of real estate and among the first in Georgia to earn the "Real Estate Property Management" REPM designation.

Chris is certified by the EPA in Lead Renovation, Repair, & Painting (RRP), a FAA licensed airframe & power plant (A&P) technician, holds a FCC license and has a strong background in construction and renovations. He has educated investors nationwide in all areas of maintenance and property management.

Chris loves the fact that his investment business is family owned and operated along with his Donna his wife who is the Broker for Solutions Realty Network. Chris & Donna are continuously sought out to speak nationwide – from Maui to New Jersey, yet are extremely approachable and available to local investors. Contact us at today at Invest@SRNhomes.com.

Chris Littleton is a real estate entrepreneur/investor. He has been associated with top realty investors for the past two decades. Considered an 'art maker' in constructing, negotiating and executing real estate deals, Chris Littleton is a maestro!

Chris Littleton Bad Deal

Rock: Tell me about your worst deal.

Chris: Real estate is not the perfect world that everybody talks about

Rock: True

Chris: I would say my worst deal was when I was just getting into real estate. I was transitioning out of the airline industry. I had extremely good credit and very good income. I ran across an investor, a wholesaler, he sold properties to investors at wholesale prices. He handled finding the properties, he handled helping you get financing for the properties, and he handled the rehabbing and getting them tenanted. He was not a broker. He was just a wholesaler. He was not quite the honest person because what we were doing was we were taking these properties, he was taking assignment fees on them, and then he was taking the rehab money. We were also financing the rehab money through the hard money loans. What happens is after I had refinanced six properties that I bought because it was a package deal I thought I was doing good. I found out that he was not a very good property manager and I found out that he was not a very good rehabber either. The rehabs were supposed to run about $10,000 apiece so we are looking at $60,000 in possible renovation money that he just pocketed. He did not spend on the properties. He was supposed to be managing properties, he was moving the tenants in rather quickly but he was moving them in from other investor's properties. Therefore, it was just compound of my properties. The tenants would move in and get a month's rent and then they would stop paying. With a little due diligence after the facts and research, I found out that he had a good operation going but he definitely was not a property manager or rehabber.

I have got all these hard money loans so then I tried to refinance out of these hard money loans and the lenders would not provide me the cash. I spent probably a year working myself out of these deals. I would say when it was all said and done with only six properties – I probably lost $40,000.

Rock: Okay

Chris: But you know what? I dusted myself off. I got out there and went back into it because what I learned from him was how to do it right because when he dropped the ball I went into action. I learned a lot from my mistakes and moved forward. His model is one that I actually used for myself when I started buying properties for $40,000 and put $15,000 into it by adding a bedroom, a bath and redoing the kitchens and then selling them for $110,000, but I was actually retailing it for $110,000.

Though there were, a few that I could not sell and I was managing myself and I managed to sell some of those all off to other investors with tenants in them, but they were really good properties. I had made the conditions good for tenants.

Eventually my investors actually wanted me to go on into the property management side of it. And I was eventually managing my own properties and it was a good fit, but first I had to settle the loss I incurred from my first mistake.

The market eventually heated up and pushed me out of the wholesale market. The houses I used to buy for $40,000 they went up to about $70,000 or $80,000 and there were no margins there for you to make money. The market rather shifted but I really worked that market for a long time and I credit that success to what I learned from my failures.

Chris Littleton Advice

Rock: What would you advice if you are a beginner investor based on your eleven years of experience?

Chris: The most important piece of real estate that you can invest in is the six inches of real estate between your ears. Get out there, learn what you are doing, and put it to practice. I find this to be true if you are generally dealing with license, real estate professionals when acquiring properties they can be a great resource to avoid some of the pitfalls. However, they are only going to be helping you on the buying side. You really have to master the art in buying in whole in today's market. You really have to master the art of rehabbing properties as well. I truly think it is a buy and hold market. Nevertheless, really, the most important thing you can do is have a real estate professional who understands the business model that you are working with or a great mentor. But avoid trying to buy properties from an individual that's so called mentoring you and look for a third party to help you evaluate those properties - a good mentor or a good real estate professional. Understand the market and educate yourself. Do your due diligence.

Rock: Great advice, so far I think the theme has been do your due diligence and be diligent about it.

Chris: Yes, I learned a valuable mistake I tell you. As I said, I learned a lot from my mistakes. However, many people could not afford that kind of mistake that I made. Therefore, I would have to say do your due diligence, educate yourself and know your market.

Rock: Thank you Chris.

Some info about Rock's services

Special Offer Free 16 minute CD

Do you have any investments or any capital that is not getting you double digits return on you investment, safely and is secured by a solid asset?

If yes, I now have a program that will pay you 20 times more in returns than you can probably get anywhere else. (NO, it's not MLM)

I have a 16 minutes CD that explains my program. Contact me if you would like it for free.

678-318-1888

www.RockTheInvestor@gmail.com

No obligation and I guarantee that your 16 minutes will be well spent.

Special $297 Offer For FREE

(Only For Readers of This Book)

Have you decided to be successful in real estate investing NOW?

Success Coaching, A Plan of Action to Freedom Through Real Estate
"A personalized coaching program that works"
By Rock Shukoor, the results coach!

I am starting a very goal oriented and systematic series of coaching sessions for my new coaching clients!

Below are short lists of action items you can plan for by working with me:

* Plan for each meeting to be one hour, 30 minutes of that is education or a case study and the other 30 minutes will be Q & A.
* Plan on having us as your accountability partner, we keep track of the results
* Plan on learning exciting and new ways of closing deals
* Plan on becoming a success.
* Plan to close deals or more deals without using your own money or credit
* Plan on working with me as I am dedicated to your success
* Plan to implement the action plan we provide you
* Plan on taking action, that is the only thing you need to do with the information I will share with you, take action!

678-318-1888

www.RockTheInvestor@gmail.com

www.HasselfreeREMentorship.com

Call and schedule a complementary, 30 minutes No obligation consulting for FREE. (Valued at $297)

My way of saying, thank you for believing in me and taking your time to read my book.

We Buy Houses
$CASH$

ANY CONDITION, ANY SITUATION, ANY AREA, ANY PRICE

Do you own an unwanted house and need to sell quickly? Are you in Foreclosure? Are you behind on Payments? Is your house Vacant? Need Repairs? Relocating? Divorce, Bad Tenant? Owe Liens? 100% Financed? Estate Sale or Fire Damage?

Is your house upside down? We can help!

Call me NOW and ask for a free report 'How to sell your house in 10 days"

Visit us at

www.WeBuyHousesCashNow.com

Or CALL NOW

(404) 419-6222

A Final Walkthrough

From the basic introduction to real – estate and the subsequent interviews that were transcribed for this book, you have to devise a plan. As they say "nobody plans to fail, but never fail to plan". Think clearly of what, how, when and who, and after you have the answers to these questions come up with a working paper and get a second and third opinion. Match your working paper against the experiences of the investors above. Do your homework every step of the way and you may just avoid the pitfalls that most real estate warriors face during their initial journey in the realm of investing. Or make it easy on yourself and work with a mentor. I offer that and I would be glad to offer you a free session to see if we can work together.

To you success,

Rateb "Rock" Shukoor

About Rateb (Rock) Shukoor
Success comes to those who dream BIG.

Rateb (Rock) Shukoor fled Afghanistan leaving behind a bitter and painful past. Oppressed by the Russians who were ruling at that time they had little to go on or to look forward to, adding to their portrait of pain, Rock Shukoor's father was imprisoned. The Russians did this due to his father's employment with the American Embassy. However, there is light in dark they say as his father's employment with the American Embassy automatically made him a US ally that allowed and paved the way for the whole family to migrate to the United States of America. It was 1989; Rock Shukoor was on American soil, and as free to dream as every other American was. Rock Shukoor's dream was big! They were so big that a blind man would be able to see it!

Rock is a very hard worker. He put himself through college by working three jobs juggling his work between McDonald's, a Flea Market and a printing shop. In 1995, He married his wife, Sahima, and they 'were blessed' with two boys, Slaymon and Paymon. The birth of his boys made him work even harder and Rock started to look for opportunities so he could provide a better life for his family. Armed with his dreams for his family, he decided to dabble with Real Estate Investing. The rest was history. Today, you can say that Rock Shukoor is living the American Dream. Real Estate has blessed him so much that he is currently living the American Dream!

For the past eleven years, Rateb "Rock" Shukoor has bought and sold hundreds upon hundreds of single-family homes in the State of Georgia. His success has drawn people to him, to seek his advice on how to become successful as Real Estate investors. A frequent speaker at investment conferences and seminars, Rateb "Rock" Shukoor is popular among other prominent real estate investors and promoters. His popularity is also the direct result of him helping thousands of investors nationwide in making profitable decisions over the years through his Hassle Free Real Estate Program. You can spend time and money to learn the necessary knowledge required in the process of becoming a property investor or you can just contact Rock Shukoor and take advantage of his Hassle Free Real Estate Partnership program. He is currently offering partnership opportunities to keen entrepreneurs who are looking for venues to make tangible profit margins. When you affiliate yourself in Rock's Hassle Free Real Estate Partnership program, he will secure your investments in ten different ways, protect you personally in four essential areas and offers a double-digit return on your investment.

For more real estate investing information, visit **www.RockTheInvestor.com** and learn more about how to get a high rate of return on your investment totally hassle free and without any headaches! **Alternatively, just dial 678-318-1888 now!**

CONCLUSION

It has been my great pleasure to have had the opportunity to sit down with these esteemed people from the real estate industry. To all of my interviewees, thank you so much for being a part of this book, thank you for your time, sharing your valuable experiences and for answering my questions so the readers can benefit from it and eventually your good and bad experiences can help them make more money, save time and headache and stay out of trouble.

To all of my readers, my heartfelt gratitude for taking the time out to read this wonderful book. It is my sincerest hope that you will not just read it but that you will also take action. Use this valuable information wisely as it is coming from investors who are running successful real estate businesses and each one of them have been in business for a minimum of 10 years or more. Cheers to your success!

To my loving family, what would I ever do without you? You are the greatest support system anyone could ever wish to have and I am 'blessed' to have you in my life. Thank you for cheering me on and supporting me in my passion. Thank you for being a part of my dreams that have come true.

To my "Dream Team", I call you 'guys' my dream team because you make my dreams come true. 'Lone rangers' do not know what they are missing, until they start working with people like you, let them be. I do not want to be one of them, and I would not know how to run a business without the help of knowledgeable and valuable people like you. So, thank you for your help, support and putting up with me through everything. From the deepest crevices of my heart, I sincerely thank you all!

Indeed, this treasure chest of a book could not be possible if not for ALL OF YOU. May we all learn from the lessons and the mistakes made that resulted to bad deals and may we be as successful as my interviewees in this book.

- Rock –

Special $297 Offer For FREE

(Only For Readers Of This Book)

I took on writing this book to provide you an overview of what are the possibilities when you decide to become a real estate investor and how to use it to grow your business. We know that you probably still have questions such as:

- Am I ready to become a real estate investor?

- Is this business for me?

- What are some pitfalls I need to know?

- Which of the many real estate buying and selling techniques or methods are appropriate in today's market?

We want to offer you an opportunity to have a 20-minute strategy session with me. I normally charge $3,000 per day individually for consulting (and the clients come to me), and what you will discover during the 20 minutes is worth much more than you can imagine.

To book your strategy session with me, please call my office 678-318-1888 and mention this special offer and my assistant will take care of the rest for you.
I will then contact you within 72 hours and if you do not hear from me, most likely, we already concluded that we could not help you based on the answers you leave on our questionnaire.

Please be patient with me because I have a very long queue for our services, and I am very selective about whom I offer my services to. After all, your success is my success.

Your Next Steps

There is a great Zen saying: "The journey is the reward." That captures the entire essence of the real estate business: it is a living, breathing thing and is constantly evolving. Your next steps depend on where you are. If you are already investing in real estate – congratulations because you are in the very small minority – just use these strategies to magnify your income.

If you have not started investing, now is the perfect time to start and then get ready for the best ride of your life. You will be pleasantly surprised at, how fast your life can change. Read the section, "**Special $297 Offer For FREE (Only For Readers Of This Book)**" and book your complimentary 1-1 strategy session with us. Call now, 678-318-1888

To a better lifestyle,

- Rateb "Rock" Shukoor-

Contact Information

Contact Rock at:

Website: www.RockTheInvestor.com

Email: RockTheInvestor@gmail.com

Benefits that I can provide include:

- Creating a roadmap that explains how to profit and live the life of a great real estate investor

- Discuss the technique and strategies that works in today's market

- What steps to take in order to start your business the proper way

- The tools necessary to run a profitable business

- Implementing the right technologies to ensure you are successful in real estate

- And much, much more

Schedule your complimentary 20 minutes strategy session by calling 678-318-1888 (for more information, see the "**Special $297 Offer For FREE (Only For Readers of This Book)**" section.